I Love
Sharks

By Steve Parker
Illustrated by John Butler

Miles Kelly
PUBLISHING

First published in 2006 by Miles Kelly Publishing Ltd
Bardfield Centre, Great Bardfield, Essex, CM7 4SL

Copyright © Miles Kelly Publishing Ltd 2006

This edition printed in 2008

2 4 6 8 10 9 7 5 3

Editorial Director Belinda Gallagher
Art Director Jo Brewer
Junior Designer Candice Bekir
Cover Artworker Stephan Davis
Production Manager Elizabeth Brunwin
Reprographics Stephan Davis

ISBN 978-1-84236-782-7

Printed in Thailand

British Library Cataloguing-in-Publication Data
A catalogue record for this book is available
from the British Library

www.mileskelly.net
info@mileskelly.net

www.factsforprojects.com

Contents

Great white shark

Sharks hunt the meat or flesh of other animals. The great white shark is the biggest, fiercest hunting shark of all. It feeds on almost any animal, from small fish to whales — and sometimes even people.

The great white's teeth are up to 8 centimetres long. There are more than 50 of them.

Great whites are so dangerous, divers who study and photograph them stay in a strong safety cage.

Jumbo shark!
The biggest great white ever weighed was 4.5 tonnes. That's as heavy as an elephant!

The great white is not white. It has a dark grey back, and a pale grey or cream belly.

Tiger shark

Some sharks have big appetites and will eat almost anything. The tiger shark eats fish, seals, dolphins, birds, other sharks, and almost anything else. Tiger sharks have also been known to swim along the coast and attack people in water that is only waist-deep.

Dustbin shark!

Tiger sharks have swallowed leftover food thrown from ships, as well as tin cans, tyres and training shoes.

The tiger shark is big and strong. It could swallow this seal in one gulp.

Tiger sharks are born with stripes on their sides. These fade as the shark gets older.

New teeth are always growing to replace the ones that wear out or snap off.

Tiger sharks are big and heavy, and weigh more than one tonne. That's the same as a small car!

Hammerhead shark

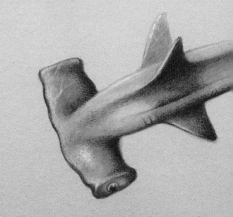

The hammerhead shark has a good sense of smell. It can smell blood in the water from a long distance away. It also has good eyesight to search for food in the water. The strange, hammer-shaped head has an eye and a nostril at either end.

Hammerheads live in schools (groups). These give the sharks safety. At night they go off to hunt alone.

Water-wings!

The 'hammer' is like an underwater wing. It helps the shark to swim well and stay up near the surface.

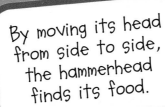

By moving its head from side to side, the hammerhead finds its food.

Hammerheads are fierce sharks with lots of sharp teeth.

Thresher shark

Sharks swish their tails to and fro, to swim fast.
The thresher shark also uses its tail like a whip,
hitting small fish to wound or stun them. Then
the thresher snaps them up to eat.

The thresher's small teeth
are shaped like triangles.
They are as sharp as knives.

Threshers eat smaller fish such as herring, mackerel and pilchard.

The thresher swims through a shoal of fish, swishing its tail to and fro. This stuns the fish.

Baby sharks
A few mother sharks, like the thresher, give birth to their babies instead of laying eggs.

11

Megamouth shark

The megamouth is a strange shark of the deep ocean. Like other sharks, it has no bones. It still has a skeleton inside its body, with parts like a skull and ribs. Instead of being made of bone, they are made of a rubbery, bendy material called cartilage.

New shark

No one had ever seen a megamouth until 1976, when one was caught near Hawaii in the Pacific Ocean.

Megamouths eat tiny shrimps and baby fish.

The megamouth's mouth is huge, about one metre across. It glows in the dark and has tiny teeth.

The loose skin and floppy fins show that the megamouth is a slow swimmer.

Whale shark

Most sharks are big. The whale shark is a giant! It is the world's biggest fish, but it is not a fierce hunter. It swims with its mouth open, trapping tiny fish and shrimps from the water in its huge mouth. Like all sharks, it cannot chew — it just swallows its food whole.

The whale shark has a spotty back and pale underside.

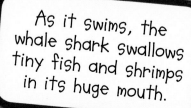

As it swims, the whale shark swallows tiny fish and shrimps in its huge mouth.

Whale sharks often lie still just under the surface of the water. No one really knows for sure why they do this.

Tiny snacks

The whale shark's food includes small fish, and shrimp-like animals called krill. Each one is about as big as your little finger.

Big sharks often have smaller fish, like these pilot fish, swimming beside them.

Port Jackson shark

Some sharks lay eggs, like the mother Port Jackson shark. She sticks them to rocks or weeds on the seabed. A few weeks later, the baby sharks hatch. They're hardly bigger than your hand. They look just like their parents — and start to hunt for food straight away.

Port Jackson sharks have a horn—like bump above each eye.

Screwy egg!

Port Jackson eggs are up to 20 centimetres long. A strange screw-shaped ridge holds the eggs among the rocks.

Saw shark

A shark's skin is covered by small scales. These are very sharp and pointed, like tiny teeth. The saw shark also has teeth outside of its mouth. These run in a row along each side of its long nose. The shark 'saws' into mud and seaweed to find fish and starfish to eat.

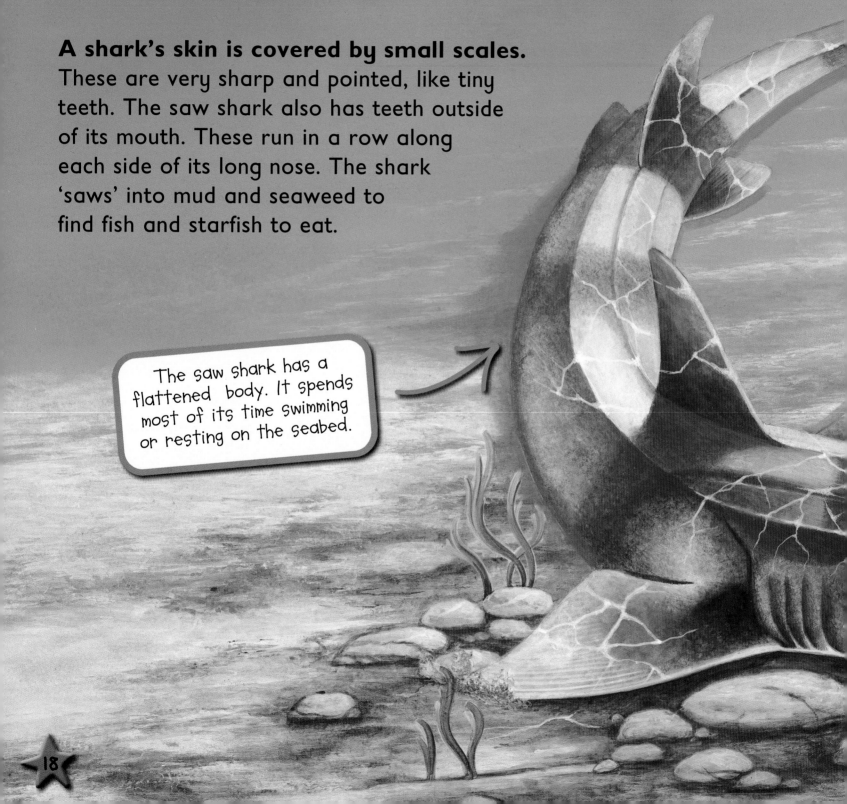

The saw shark has a flattened body. It spends most of its time swimming or resting on the seabed.

This shark prefers to live in deeper water. It isn't often seen near the shore.

Be a saw shark!
Make a saw shark mask from card. Ask an adult to help you cut out the saw-shaped nose.

On each side of the snout is a long feeler. It wriggles like a finger in the mud to find food.

Teeth along the nose are as sharp as a saw.

Wobbegong

Why are most sharks pale grey or light blue? These colours help to hide the shark from its prey. The wobbegong, or carpet shark, has green, yellow and brown skin. This helps it hide among the rocks and seaweed on the seabed. It grabs passing fish to eat.

The wobbegong lies very still on the seabed waiting for a meal. It may not move for hours.

The shark blends in with its surroundings. This is called camouflage.

Wobbegongs prefer to live in shallow water. Some get stuck in big rockpools when the tide goes out.

Carpet shark!

Get some patches of paper the same colour as your carpet. Tape them to some old clothes and lie on the carpet. Are you camouflaged?

White-tipped reef shark

Sharks don't just swim and hunt. Some like to have a rest. White-tipped reef sharks sleep in caves or under rocks during the day. At night, they go their separate ways and swim off to hunt for fish, crabs and lobsters.

These sharks may be still by day, but if a tasty fish comes near – they wake up in a flash!

The white-tipped fins make this shark easy to recognize.

Close eyes!
When a shark attacks, a special piece of skin slides down to protect its eyes.

The big fin, on the side of the body helps the shark steer as it swims.

Fun facts

Great white shark After eating a large meal of seals or penguins, great whites may not feed again for a month or two.

Tiger shark This shark gets its name from the stripes it is born with, which fade as it grows older.

Hammerhead shark One type of hammerhead shark must swim all the time, or else it will drown.

Thresher shark This shark is a strong swimmer and sometimes leaps out of the water.

Megamouth shark First discovered in 1976, the megamouth eats only tiny shrimps.

Whale shark Mother whale sharks can give birth to hundreds of live young.

Port Jackson shark The Port Jackson can eat and breathe at the same time, it doesn't have to keep swimming.

Saw shark Most sharks have five pairs of gill slits, but the saw shark has six.

Wobbegong Divers have been known to step on wobbegongs by mistake, as they're so well disguised on the seabed.

White-tipped reef shark These sharks are lazy during the day, but they come to life at night to hunt.